My Dreaming is the Christmas Bird

The Story of Irene Jimmy
as told to

Sarah Fitzherbert

with photographs by
Howard Birnstihl

BOOKSHELF

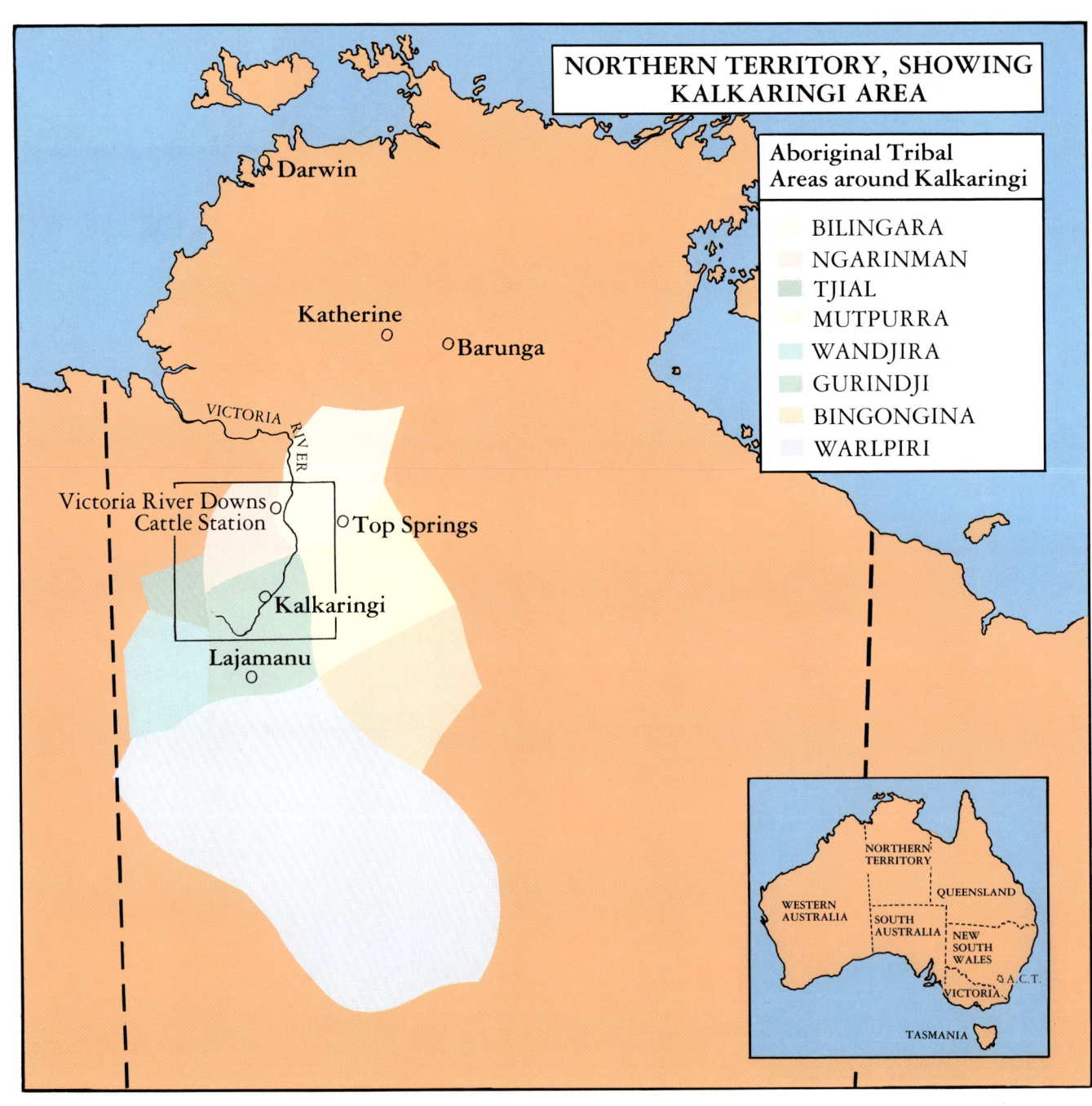

NORTHERN TERRITORY, SHOWING
KALKARINGI AREA

Aboriginal Tribal
Areas around Kalkaringi

BILINGARA
NGARINMAN
TJIAL
MUTPURRA
WANDJIRA
GURINDJI
BINGONGINA
WARLPIRI

Darwin

Katherine

Barunga

VICTORIA
RIVER

Victoria River Downs
Cattle Station

Top Springs

Kalkaringi

Lajamanu

NORTHERN
TERRITORY

WESTERN
AUSTRALIA

QUEENSLAND

SOUTH
AUSTRALIA

NEW
SOUTH
WALES

A.C.T.

VICTORIA

TASMANIA

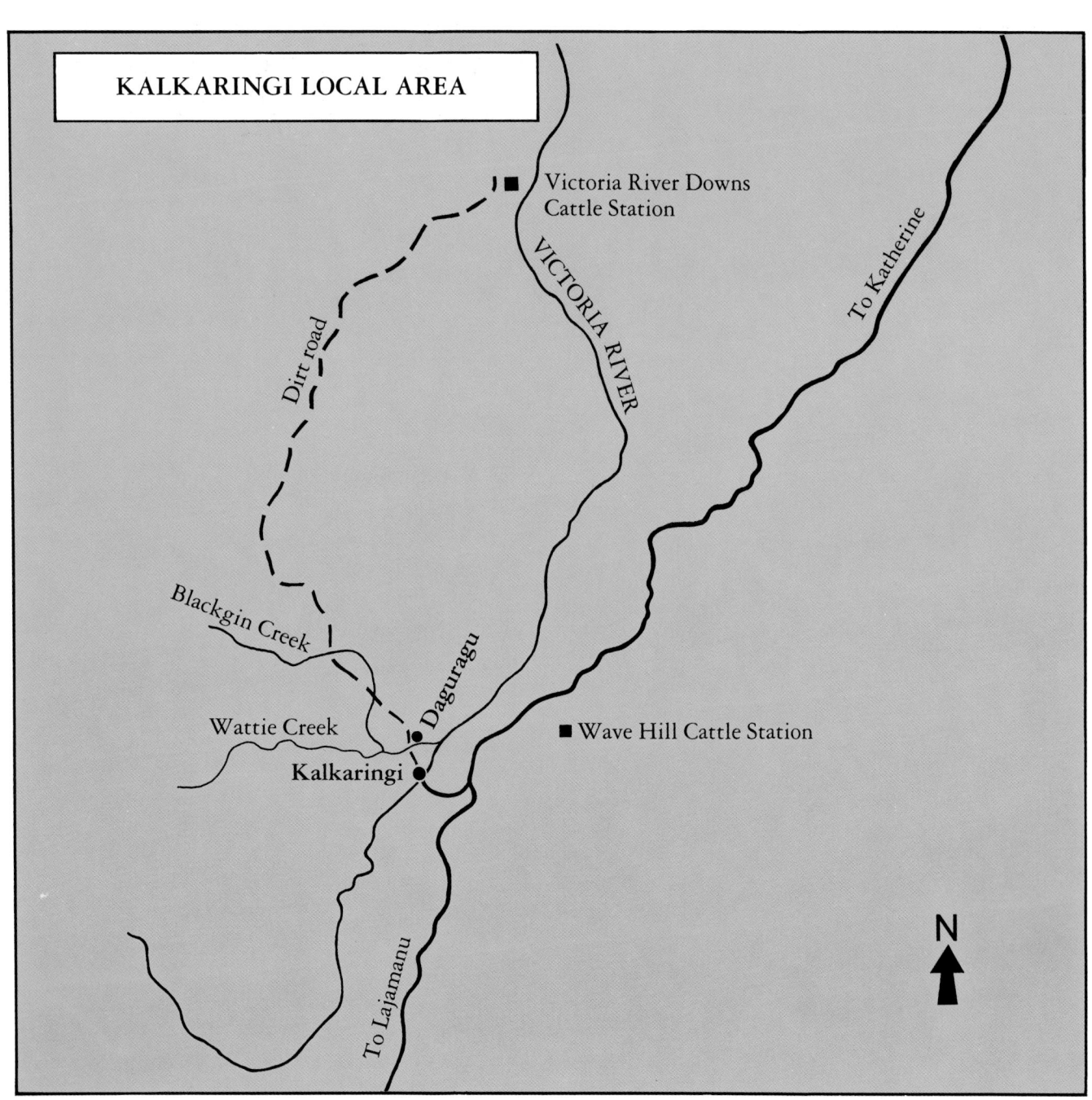

KALKARINGI LOCAL AREA

Victoria River Downs
Cattle Station

VICTORIA RIVER

To Katherine

Dirt road

Blackgin Creek

Daguragu

Wattie Creek

■ Wave Hill Cattle Station

Kalkaringi

To Lajamanu

N

For Amanda Butler

PRONUNCIATION GUIDE

These rules will help you to say our Gurindji words.

1 The stress is on the first syllable.

2 There is only one way to say each vowel:
"a" is like the "ar" in "bark"
"e" is like the "ee" in "feet"
"u" is like the "u" in "put".

3 "ng" is like the sound on the end of "sing".

4 "rr" is a bit like "d" in English.

NOTE:
The Christmas bird is the channel-billed cuckoo.

The information and photographs in this book
are reproduced by permission of the Gurindji
people of Kalkaringi and Daguragu.

Contents

Introduction

My name is Irene Jimmy. I am eleven years old. I live with my family in the Northern Territory of Australia. My town is Kalkaringi, 460 kilometres south-west of Katherine on the Victoria River. Kalkaringi and Daguragu, ten kilometres down the road on Wattie Creek, are where the Gurindji people live.

The other kids and I love to hear stories of the early days before the *kartiya* (white people) came, and of the times when the Gurindji lived at Old Wave Hill Cattle Station.

Kalapiti, an elder of my people, tells us his story of the flood in 1924, when his father Tinker made the rain and the first Wave Hill Station homestead was washed away:

Long time ago when Kalapiti small, the people were camping at Lipanangku near Victoria River. River was nearly dry – just small puddles of dirty water. No grass for horses and bullocks – they were poor. *Kartiya* boss, Mr Rankin, he make a bet with Tinker he couldn't make rain because it was the wrong time.

Tinker, he went to Wilki Yard, 'Seven Mile'. He dive under the water in the early morning. He stay under looking for old *Kurraj*, the rainbow serpent, until lunchtime. He look in all the deep pockets right down at the bottom of the waterhole. He found different *Kurraj*.

At last he found the old woman snake. She come from Catfish Waterhole. They spoke for long time. Tinker explained how there been no rain. The *Kurraj* agreed to make rain. Tinker put four little rainstones in the serpent's mouth. The serpent swallowed them right down. She licked Tinker like a dog.

Four clouds came up and melted together and spread out. It rained four days and four nights. You couldn't see the sun. Floodwater came and the camp had to be shifted by buggy up to Jinbarrak. Wave Hill Station homestead washed away.

Kalapiti

The station homestead was built again at Jinbarrak, on higher ground. This was where my mum and dad grew up and lived with the rest of our people before all the Gurindji left Wave Hill Station.

Now I'll tell you my story of the Gurindji. I've learnt most of it from the old people's stories – stories about the early days, and about life on Wave Hill Station and in the Daguragu camp. The rest I know because it is about my own life in Kalkaringi today.

My Family

I have seven brothers and two sisters. Two of my brothers are married and have children of their own. Derek is 26 and lives and works in Kununurra. Patrick is 24 and works in the settlement as a trained health worker. He helps to run the health clinics at Kalkaringi and Daguragu. Then there's Phillip who is 20 and is training to be a teacher. Warren is 18 and works as a stockman on a cattle station a long way off, so we don't see him very often. Colin who is 16, and my big sister Carol who is 14, are away at high school. Colin goes to Yirara College in Alice Springs and Carol goes to Kormilda College in Darwin. They come home during the school holidays.

I am the oldest of the children who still live at home. I am in Year 6 at Kalkaringi School. My little sister Carolyn is 9 and is in Year 2. Then I have two little brothers, Kerry who is 6, and Dameul who is 3. Kerry is in Year 1 and Dameul goes to afternoon pre-school.

Our family has quite a few pets. We have a black dog called *Naburu*, a brown dog called *Nangari*, a cat and three ducks, and we mind some ducks for other people as well.

Our parents, Jimmy Wave Hill and Biddy, grew up when the Gurindji lived on Wave Hill Station. Dad was a stockman and Mum sometimes worked at the homestead.

When the Gurindji left Wave Hill Station and everyone came to live in the settlement, Dad worked for the Daguragu Community Council. He cut down trees to make fences and drove a backhoe to help build all the houses. Now he makes traditional shields. Mum spends most of her time looking after us kids but she also makes *kuturu* (fighting sticks for ceremonies) and *kawala* (painted oval bark cradles to carry babies in).

Opposite: Me and some of my family – from left to right, Colin, Kerry, Dameul, Mum, Me (in front), Carol and Dad
Below: Mum bathing Patrick's son

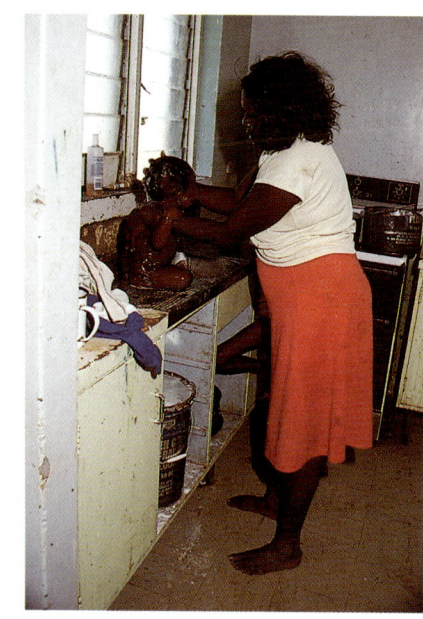

Above: The kids' bedroom
Right: Our house

Carolyn, Kerry, Dameul and I are not the only kids who live in our house. Our cousins Margaret and Magdalene live here too. All of us young kids sleep in one big room at the end of the house. When Carol is home she sleeps there as well. We have a whole row of big mattresses on the floor. Mum and Dad sleep in a room of their own, and when my older brothers are home they sleep in the other small room.

In our house we also have a living room, kitchen, bathroom and laundry, and louvre windows and ceiling fans to help keep the house cool. Mum usually cooks on the stove in the kitchen but when we have firewood she often cooks outside.

Our Land

Gurindji country is hot and dry. We have three seasons. From late December, when the rains come, until April is *yipungka*, the rainy (or wet) season. This is when daytime temperatures are usually above 40°C in the shade. Most of the rain falls in December and January, and we get about 400-500 millimetres.

No rain falls between May and August and we call this *makurru*, the cold season. It is still hot for some of this time, but it is cooler in June and July when it's usually 25-35°C during the daytime and the nights can be cold (15°C and below). In June and July the council brings us firewood to help us keep warm at night. That is when we often cook outside.

Gurindji country in the dry season

From September till it starts raining in December is *parunga*, the dry season. You wouldn't believe how hot it gets in our classrooms at this time of year.

The land around Kalkaringi is mostly flat, wide grassland with small trees dotted about, but there are some low hills just to the east of the town. We call these hills the *Karungkani* and there are many stories about them.

Further out from the settlement there is all kinds of country. To the south there is hilly spring country where clear, fresh water gushes up from deep underground all year round. Big fig trees grow around these springs and keep them shady and cool on hot days. There are also grassland plains and patches of scrub, and even bits of forest country. A few flat-topped mountains rise out of the flat plains and glow red in the morning and evening light. Along the river and watercourses are deep rocky gorges with tall red cliffs and big old paperbarks. Our country has many different faces.

You see a lot of changes from one season to the next. By the end of the dry season the ground is hard and dusty, the grass thins out and goes yellow and the countryside looks bare. But when the rains come at the beginning of the wet it all starts to change. Grass suddenly grows on the hard ground and you can see all sorts of small flowering plants. The insects hatch and the birds begin to nest, and the place is soon full of wildlife. The country begins to look green and lush.

Opposite: The spring at Seale Yard is one of our favourite places on a hot day. Big fig trees make it shady and cool
Above left: Gurindji country at the end of the wet
Above right: "Fourteen Mile" waterhole at the end of the wet

The Town where I Live

Above: Kalkaringi street
Opposite: Kalkaringi from the air

Kalkaringi is a much smaller town than Katherine. A bitumen highway comes from Katherine and goes down to Daguragu, but all the other roads are dirt. There are only a few streets and they don't need names. Instead all the houses have a number. Our house is Number 42. There are about fifty houses in Kalkaringi. About fifteen of them are for the *kartiya* who live in the settlement and the rest are for the *ngumpit* (Aboriginal people). Mainly they are made from fibro cement but some are brick.

Most of the Aboriginal houses are like our house. They have kitchens, bathrooms and laundries, and louvres and ceiling fans. Down at Daguragu there are not so many houses and they have tin walls and concrete floors. Most have no kitchens, bathrooms or laundries. The Daguragu people cook on fires and eat outside, and they wash their clothes under the taps at the community shower blocks.

In Kalkaringi we also have a school, a health clinic, a police station, the Aboriginal Council Office, a church, a power house, a water tower and pump house, a mechanics' workshop, and a general store, take-away and service station.

Our Food

The Gurindji still like to eat bush foods but there is not enough wild food around Kalkaringi for all the people to eat every day. In the early days people walked in small family groups all over Gurindji land following the food supply. The people hunted kangaroos and wallabies and caught big goannas and pythons. They gathered fruit and nuts and dug up yams as they went from place to place.

Then for over eighty years, after the *kartiya* came into our country, the Gurindji had to go to live and work on Wave Hill Station because it soon covered all of our tribal land. That's where we began to eat beef, flour and sugar and to drink tea.

Now we have some of our land back but we can't live in the old way any more. These days we live in one place and have learnt to drive cars instead of walking. Only a few of our people have cars, so we hardly ever go far from the settlement to look for wild foods. The land around the settlement is nearly hunted out and all those years of cattle grazing have changed it, so that wild foods don't grow as they used to. Anyway, it is much easier to go shopping at the store, so these days we eat mainly *kartiya* foods.

We walk down to the Kalkaringi store to buy tinned beef, flour, sugar, tea, oranges and apples, potatoes and carrots, milk and jam. The food's expensive because it's brought in by refrigerated truck from Katherine. Next to the store is a take-away where we can get roast chicken and chips, hamburgers, steak sandwiches, ham and pickle sandwiches, cheese sandwiches and fruit. The take-away also sells canned drinks, ice-creams and chocolate bars out of the freezer.

There's another big store down at Daguragu. Every second

Below: Ngarin *(beef) cooking on the fire outside*
Opposite: Shopping at the Daguragu store

Wednesday afternoon when the cheques come in, the Daguragu store is full of people buying food.

We don't like to buy *ngarin* (meat) from the store because it's too expensive. We like it when someone brings in a "killer". Every two weeks some of the men go out hunting the wild cattle that roam around Kalkaringi. Each hunter brings in one killer and the meat is shared by his whole family – usually a lot of people. You should see the big feasts we have when the killer comes in! Most people don't have refrigerators, so the meat has to be eaten in a few days.

Sometimes Dad or one of my uncles or brothers shoots a *jikpan* (wild turkey) out on the plain. The rest of us kids help to pluck the bird and then it is cooked on the open fire or in the oven. It tastes great!

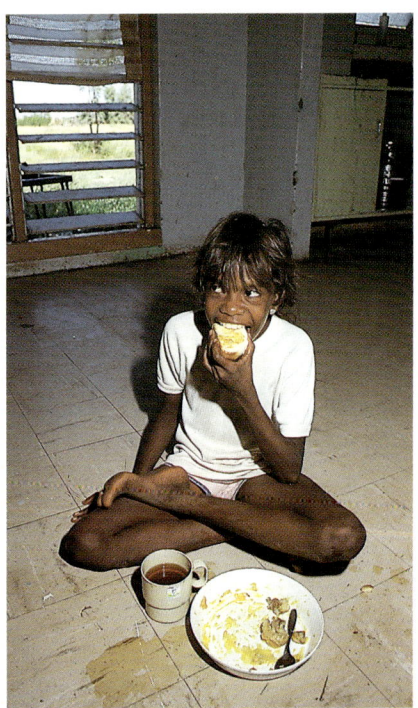

*Above: We often have vegetable stew
for lunch, with damper and tea
Right: Plucking a wild turkey*

At home Mum makes damper in the oven or in a big oiled frypan on top of the stove, unless there is enough wood for a fire outside. For lunch she cooks up tasty meat and vegetable stews in a big saucepan, and we always have a big pot of strong black tea as well.

In our spare time, though, one of our favourite things to do is to go out with the women along the river to fish, swim and look for bush tucker.

The Victoria River is part of our everyday lives. In the wet season the river fills very quickly and sometimes even rises to the top of the bridge. All the billabongs are full of water and we can fish anywhere along the river and collect lots of different bush foods.

After the wet the river falls but there is still plenty of water for several months. Then, during the dry season, the river slowly dries up until only the deepest waterholes are left. These waterholes usually have water right through the dry, so we visit them often to swim and fish. They all have names. "Four Mile", "Seven Mile" and "Ten Mile" are south along the river, and "Policeman's Hole" and "Fourteen Mile" are north. As the river dries up, the fish are trapped in these waterholes so it is easy to catch them. We spend a lot of time fishing for black and silver bream, catfish, pike and barramundi.

"Seven Mile" waterhole in the dry

We walk to a good fishing spot

Sometimes my family goes out with a big mob of people to a waterhole for the whole day. We buy fishing lines at the store. They have one hook and a small sinker. When we get to the river we look for bait. We turn over stones in the shallow parts of the river looking for freshwater shrimps and small catfish. We hunt for grasshoppers in the long grass and find beetle grubs in the branches of trees. We hunt for frogs in the sand along the river bank. When we find them we kill them straight away by flinging them to the ground or dropping stones on them. Black bream, silver bream and catfish like beetle grubs, grasshopper or meat cut up into small pieces. Barramundi like frogs.

We dig frogs from the sand for bait to catch barramundi

Grasshoppers make good bait too

Setting up camp under the paperbarks at "Ten Mile"

Right: First I have to untangle my line
Below: This is a bream, but it's only small

Sometimes we see freshwater crocodiles out on the river but they are *minyirri* (shy) and swim away when they see us. There are no saltwater crocodiles down our way.

My friends and I are clever at catching fish. We know just how much bait to put on the hook, how to cast the line and how to snare the fish once they are nibbling at the bait. To catch bream we throw the line out into the middle of the river and pull it in just fast enough to keep the bait on top of the water. The bream comes up to the surface to take the bait. For barramundi it is best to have a boat and go out into the middle of the river where the water is deep. We hold the line very still.

While we are fishing, some of the women hunt for turtles in the mud at the bottom of the river.

When we have caught enough fish for a good meal we break off green sticks from the trees and thread the fish onto them, usually through the eyes, then we carry them back along the river to our camp in the shade of some huge paperbarks.

Fishing

Below left: Dad cuts an oval of bark from the white gum to mix the damper on
Below right: We put the cooked damper on a bed of fresh green leaves
Opposite: The bream is cooked slowly on the coals

By the time we get back, the women have a good fire going and a big billy on the boil. People are making *mangarri* (damper). Mum and Dad often make *mangarri* out in the bush. Dad cuts an oval piece of bark from the trunk of the white gum. We bring self-raising flour and water from the river and mix it on the bark until it is a soft dough. Then we make it into small flat cakes and put them on the coals of the fire. It cooks in about twenty minutes and it is very good to eat. Sometimes we bring jam to spread on it.

The small fish are also cooked on the coals, first one side and then the other. Turtles are cooked on their backs so that they roast in their own shells. We cook barramundi in a special way. We gut the fish and fill it with heated stones. We close it up again by threading a fine stick through the flesh, then wrap the fish in paperbark. We dig a trench and put in some hot coals from the fire, then put the fish in the trench and cover it with more coals. It cooks slowly like this and tastes very good.

Sometimes we catch a *kirrawa* (goanna) out by the river and cook it in the same way as the barramundi. Goanna beef is the nicest bush tucker, apart from sugar bag.

Above left: Coming down from the nampula *tree*
Above right: There is plenty of nampula *for everyone*
Right: Pounding the nampula *to get the nuts*

In the wet season and just after it there are many bush foods to collect along the river. The women often take us out to look for fruit and nuts. The most common fruit around here are *ngamanypurru* (konkleberries), *karraj-karraj* (bush berries), *muyung* (bush plums), *kilipi* (bush figs), *nampula* (bush nuts), *kitpan* (melons) and *kamara* (yams). *Muyung* and *ngamanypurru* are our favourite fruit in the early part of the wet season.

Left: Nampula *(left) and* kitpan *(right)*
Above: This kitpan *is too green to eat*

Nampula have a hard shell around the small nut inside. To break them open we put them one by one on a flat stone and then pound them with another stone until the shell breaks open and the nut falls out. It takes a long time to get a handful of nuts.

Kitpan grow on long vines which run along the ground and when they turn yellow they are very juicy and good to eat, but we can't eat them when they are green because they make us sick.

We also like to eat the roots and seeds of the *mintaaraaj* (waterlily). *Mintaaraaj* grow along the edges of the billabongs when there is plenty of water. The women wade along the edge and reach down into the water to pull up the roots. We cook them slowly on the ashes of the fire then peel off the burnt outer layer. The *kartiya* kids at school say they taste like chestnuts, but I've never tried a chestnut.

Underwater along the edges of the billabongs the women sometimes find *tuku* (freshwater mussels). We cook them in the ashes too.

This page, clockwise: Roots and flower of the mintaaraaj; *This witchetty grub will be slowly roasted on the coals; One of my friends finds a plover's egg*
Opposite: The old women wade in the water to pull up the mintaaraaj *roots*

Above left: Amy uses a sharp tomahawk to cut open the bees' nest
Above right: When the wood comes away, we scoop the sugar bag out with our hands
Opposite, top left: A handful of sugar bag
Opposite, top right: Sugar bag is our favourite bush food
Opposite, bottom: One of my friends finds some martiya *up in an acacia tree*

But the bush food that my friends and I like best of all is *ngarlu* (sugar bag). The wild bees make their nests in the trunks and branches of trees not too far from the river. We love to go out with the older women, who know how to find them. There are all sorts of trees that the bees like to nest in. We pick one out and stand under it and watch very closely for a few minutes. The wild bees are very tiny and sometimes the hives are quite high up so it is not easy to see them. The entrance to the hive is just a tiny hole in the trunk or branch and we have to watch to see just one or two bees flying to the same place on the tree. Once we have found the hole we listen very carefully for the low buzzing sound that the bees make down inside the nest. The women use a small, sharp axe to cut away the trunk or branch of the tree below the hole. The wild bees have hardly any sting so it's quite safe. It takes a while to cut open the hive but when the wood comes away the honey starts to run out in a thick, golden stream. We all run to catch it in our cups and tins and scrape all the honeycomb and pollen out with our hands. It has a strong, sweet taste and it's very hard not to eat it all before we get

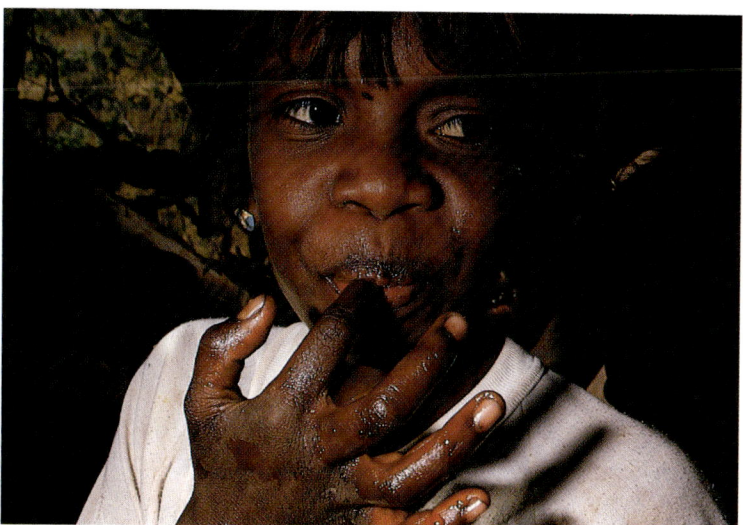

back to camp. Sometimes we find three or four hives close to each other on the same day and then there is plenty of sugar bag for everyone.

It's fun looking for *martiya* too. This is bush chewing gum, the sap of a kind of acacia tree up our way. The women like to chew bush chewing tobacco which grows along the watercourses.

Bush Medicines

The old women teach us about the bush medicines

We have a health clinic at Kalkaringi but the people still like to use the traditional cures. While we are out with the women they tell us all about the bush medicines.

When someone has a bad cold the women pick *manyanyi* (bush tea) from along the river. They dry it out and then pour boiling water over it and the sick person drinks it. *Manyanyi* is also used to put on sores.

If someone has diarrhoea they mix dirt from an anthill with water, warm it up and give it to the sick person to drink. Mothers breastfeeding their babies drink this too if their babies have diarrhoea.

The best cure for vomiting is to hold the sick person in the smoke of a fire made with a special sort of leaf.

Our Dreaming

The older women teach us about bush foods and bush medicines but it is the old men who tell us stories of the early days, of the *Kurraj* dreaming when the rainbow snake travelled through our land and made the Victoria River. They take us out to show us the places where the rainbow snake and all the other spirits of the Dreamtime stopped on their journeys and left their marks. These places are very important to the Gurindji. There are over two hundred of these sites on our land, mostly along the river – waterholes, billabongs, rock holes, steep escarpments and gorges. Some of them are sacred and can be visited only by certain people at particular times.

We believe that the Dreamtime spirits gave us the job of looking after the land and watching over these special places. If we don't do our job well there will be big trouble with the spirits. We must always be careful not to offend the Dreamtime spirits.

All the special places on Gurindji land have *kuning* (dreamings). The Victoria River is the *Kurraj* (rainbow snake) dreaming. Daguragu is built on the path of the *ngamanypurru* (konkleberry) dreaming. Seale Gorge is on the *palngarawuny* (poison fish) dreaming. Old Wave Hill Station was built on the *karu* (children) dreaming. Every Gurindji has a dreaming, and some of us have more than one. Our dreaming is a special relationship with the land, the plants, birds or animals, which we have from the time we are born. Every dreaming has its own songs and ceremonies. My dreaming is *kurawuraka*, the Christmas bird.

Smiler Kata is one of the old men who likes to teach us about the early days

Our Traditional Ways

Seale Gorge is a very special place not far from Daguragu where we often go with the old men, Kalapiti and Kata. They like to take groups of us kids out there to learn the traditional ways. All along Seale Gorge are the rock paintings, which all tell different stories. The drawings have special meanings and special powers. If someone does something wrong, like breaking a promise of marriage or marrying someone with the wrong skin name, the person who has been wronged, or that person's family, can go out to Seale Gorge and draw the wrongdoer up on the rock with a bone of *palngarawuny* (the poison fish) stuck in the body. The wrongdoer soon gets sick and dies unless the person who drew the picture on the rock comes back and rubs off the drawing of the fish bone.

Above: This painting shows someone falling from the top of the cliff
Right: Seale Gorge
Opposite: We like to look at the rock paintings

There is also an old bloodwood tree out near the gorge which Kalapiti showed us. Long ago one of our ancestors cut off a great oval-shaped piece of bark, painted someone up on the tree underneath with a fish bone in the side, then nailed the bark back on. It is still there today, a very old tree with a painting on it.

Out in the rock ledges of Seale Gorge is also an old Gurindji burial ground. Kalapiti tells us that in the early days when someone died they put the body on a platform up in a tree for one year. Then they took down the bones, cleaned them up and polished them with red ochre. They wrapped the polished bones in paperbark and put them up in a rock ledge in the gorge, in a "home place" where the family could come and look after them. Once a year, in the cooler months, the family would come and polish the bones. The people don't do this any more but there are still some of those old bones up in the gorge.

Out there at Seale Gorge is also a place where we can find old flintstones from the early days. Kalapiti tells us how our ancestors used *yirrijkaji* wood hardened in the fire to make flintstones out of rock, then used the flintstones to sharpen their *milarrang* (spears).

Our ancestors made spears from yirrijkaji *wood and flintstones*

Yirrijkaji was used to make spears too. Dad learnt to hunt and make spears when he was young. His grandfather taught him how to use the heat of the fire to straighten the wood, and how to track and kill the animals. But our people don't hunt with spears any more. They use rifles these days.

Left and below: The women paint us up for dancing

Sometimes big groups of us kids go out with the old men and women to learn dancing. We take white and red paint from the school and the old people paint us up for a corroboree. Kalapiti and Kata play the boomerangs and sticks, and sing. One of the old women leads us girls and shows us how to turn and stamp and move our feet while the boys sit and watch. Then the girls all sit and watch while one of the old men leads the boys in their dance. Afterwards we all go and jump into the river to cool down and wash off the paint. These are days when we really have a good time.

Right: One of the old women leads the girls in the dance (I am second from the left)
Below: The boys wait their turn

Our Ceremonies and Customs

After the first big rain of the wet every year it is time for ceremonies among the Gurindji. Many different sorts of ceremonies are held, but particularly the initiation ceremonies when young boys between eleven and fourteen years old are prepared for manhood. For several days before the main ceremonies is *Pantimi* (the women's dance) when the women all get painted up and dance every evening. Sometimes the dances go on all night. Then the boys go through days of ceremonies to separate them from the women of their family and teach them the ways of men. Afterwards they are taken away to a secret camp to discuss men's business. They go on learning men's business for many years after that. Girls are not initiated but when we reach puberty we are allowed to go to secret women's ceremonies where men and boys are forbidden.

Our names

Gurindji people all have a first and second name (*kartiya* names), an Aboriginal name and a skin name.

For our second name we usually have our father's first name. My father's name is Jimmy Wave Hill, so my name is Irene Jimmy and we are all known as the Jimmy kids.

Gurindji families are very big but this is not just because we have lots of aunts, uncles and cousins. It is also because we all belong to a skin group which is like a much bigger family. There are eight skin groups and each has a name for men and a name for women. When a baby is born it gets a skin name from its mother but this is not the same as her skin name. It works like this: Mum's skin name is *Nangala*, so all the girls in our family are *Nalyirri* (or *Nyanyi* for short) and all the boys are *Japalyi*. Mum often calls me *Nyanyi* instead of Irene. Our grandmother (mother's mother) is *Nangari*, and when I have children they will be *Nawula* (for girls) and *Juluma* (for boys).

This means that all Gurindji women called *Nangala* are my mothers and all women called *Nalyirri* are my sisters. All the *Nangari* are my grandmothers. All the men called *Japalyi* are my brothers. So I have lots of grandmothers, mothers, sisters and brothers as well as my real family.

Our mother Biddy is a Nangala. *That means that my sisters and I are* Nalyirri *and our brothers are* Japalyi

Marriage

There are rules too about which skin names can marry and which are forbidden to marry. Because I am a *Nalyirri* I am supposed to marry a *Japarta*, but I have a second and third choice.

However, it is forbidden for me to marry a *Japalyi*, my brothers' skin. Once we are grown up I am not even supposed to talk to a *Japalyi*. The strict rules for marriage are not followed so closely any more but some marriages are still wrong.

GURINDJI SKIN NAMES, SISTER AND BROTHER SKINS

Nangari	Jangari
Nangala	Jangala
Nalyirri (Nyanyi)	Japalyi
Namija	Jungurra
Nanaku	Janama
Nimarra	Japarta
Nawula	Juluma
Nampijina	Jampijina

RELATIONSHIPS BETWEEN DIFFERENT SKIN GROUPS

Female skin names (in yellow) begin with *N*. Male skin names (in green) begin with *J*. Joined boxes show correct marriage. Arrows point from the marriage partners to the children.

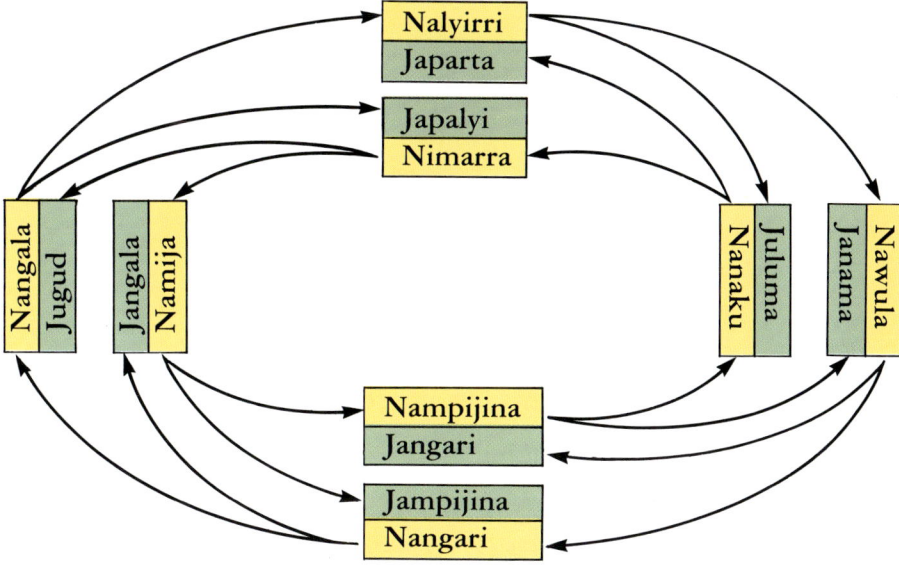

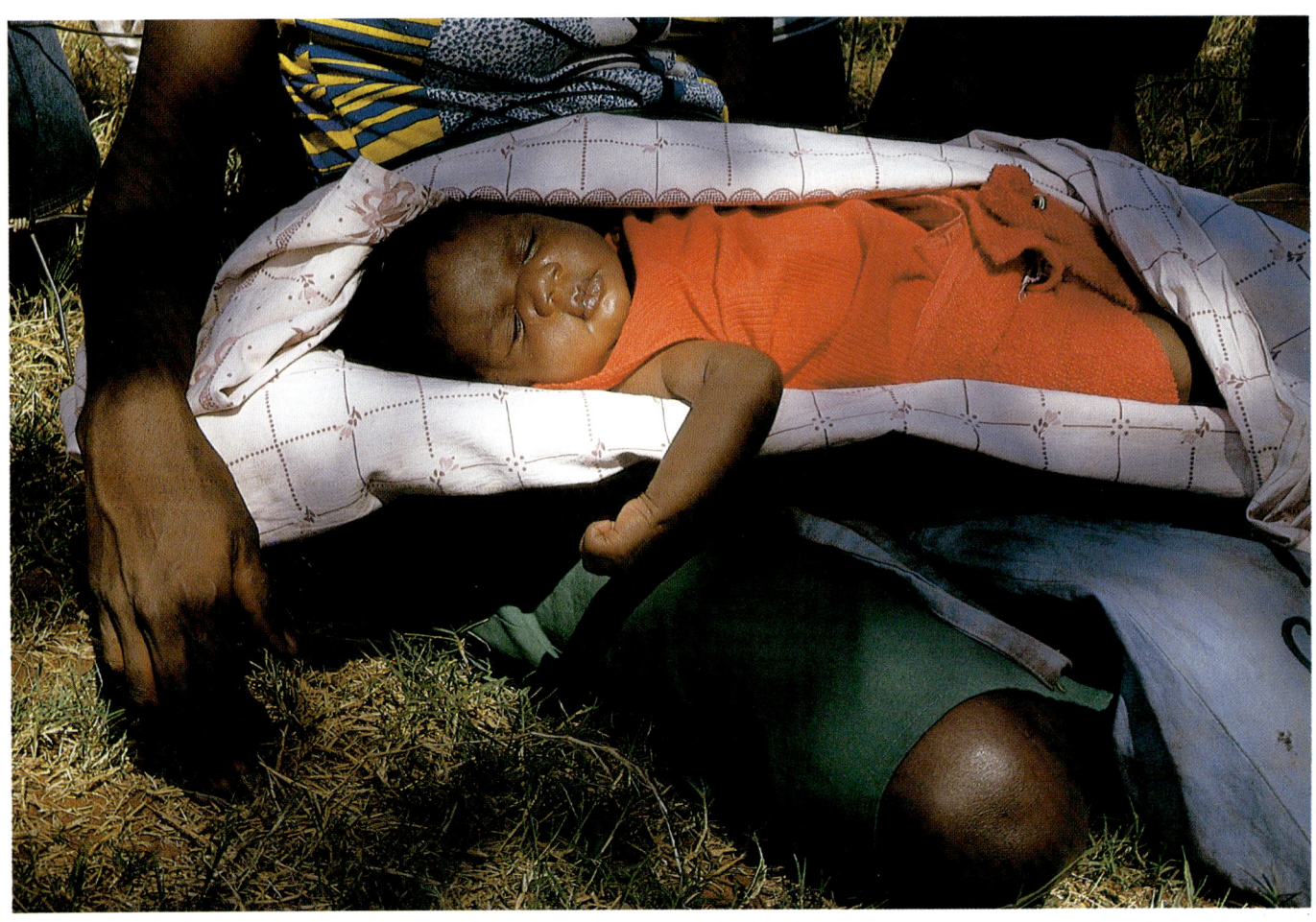

A baby girl asleep in a kawala.
*Baby girls are not always promised at
birth these days*

In the early days, when a girl baby was born she was promised in marriage to an older man. When she turned thirteen or fourteen she went to live in the old man's house to look after him. Gurindji men are allowed to have more than one wife, so the man's older wives looked after the children while the young wife looked after the old man. When the old man died it was arranged for the young wife to marry a younger man. Things are changing these days, and baby girls are not always promised to a husband at birth any more.

"Kulum mulung"

There is another important rule among the Gurindji that has to do with names. When someone dies the people are very sad, and for a long time after, sometimes many years, you are not allowed to say that person's name. You can write the name but not say it. Anybody else who has the same name has to be called Kulum (short for kulum mulung, meaning "can't say") for that time.

I have been called Kulum since someone with my name died a year ago. My brother Colin has been called Kulum for a long time.

The Old Days at Wave Hill Station

The walk-off

The old men teach us a lot about the traditional ways of our people, but they also like to tell us about their lives on Wave Hill Station and about the "walk-off", a very important event in the recent history of the Gurindji. To understand this story we need to know what happened over a hundred years ago.

The Gurindji have lived around this part of the Victoria River for many thousands of years. In the mid-1800s *kartiya* began to come into our land to look for good grazing country. The first cattle came into the area in 1883 and Wave Hill Cattle Station was set up. Wave Hill Cattle Station and other stations in the area grew until they swallowed up all the Gurindji land, so the Gurindji had to go to live and work on the cattle stations. In 1914 a big English meat company bought Wave Hill Station and by 1940 it had spread to 15,944 square kilometres. Because of our skills in hunting and tracking, our knowledge of the country and the way we learnt to handle horses at Wave Hill Station, our men were soon known as top stockmen and cattlemen. The women of our group cooked and cleaned at the Station. Our people worked hard for their wages of flour, sugar and tea.

In 1967 the Gurindji elders agreed that we should not work for flour, sugar and tea any more, so all the people walked off Wave Hill Station and made a permanent camp at Daguragu.

For eight years the Gurindji refused to leave Daguragu. We wanted to stay in our traditional area, close to our sacred sites. The town of Kalkaringi was built for us by the Government, but not many people moved to live there at first. During this time the Gurindji made a land claim to the Australian Government, the first Aboriginal land claim in Australian history.

In 1975 the Federal Government recognised our claim and gave back to the Gurindji part of Wave Hill Station west of the Victoria River, 3240 square kilometres of land. We could again have ownership of the land and decide our own futures. In a hand-over ceremony at Daguragu, Vincent Lingiari accepted a handful of Gurindji soil from Prime Minister Gough Whitlam. It was a very important moment for the Gurindji.

Now there are about 250 people, mostly Gurindji but also some Warlpiri, Mutpurra and Bilingara people, living in the settlement at Kalkaringi, and about 350 at Daguragu.

Other stories

Old Mick Rangiari, president of the Daguragu Community Council, likes to talk about the old days at Wave Hill Station. He used to work as a police tracker. The Gurindji were often employed as trackers by the *kartiya* because we are very clever at following the tracks of animals, people and vehicles over the dry, stony country. There are still Gurindji employed as police trackers in Kalkaringi today.

One day Mick had a bad fall from a horse and damaged his leg, so he couldn't work as a tracker any more. This is the story he told us about how it happened:

Mick Rangiari

    " In the early days when Mick work as police tracker, police woman said to Mick, 'You have to get some mail from Wave Hill Station.' We brought horses to the yard. Mick grab one horse and put the saddle on. Jumped on horse and went to the Station. Got there at 10.00 am, stayed until late afternoon, 4.00 pm, then had to come back with mail and meat for the rest of the police trackers. Horse was too frightened of meat – the smell. He bolted away. Mick put meat in fork of tree to quiet horse, but couldn't leave it – needed it for police trackers. Had to come back for it. Grabbed it and put it on pommel of saddle. Two miles from Station, horse bolted again. Hit a rock and fell down. Couple of rolls. Mick still in saddle. Pretty bad. Couldn't get up all night.

One old man came driving with three old women about 4.00 next afternoon.

'How long you bin here?' he ask.

'Since last night.'

'I got to get you to Wave Hill Station.'

That old man went back and told Mick's family. They all come out footwalk. Manager came with vehicle. Next day police came with Dr Benton in a plane. Took Mick to Katherine and then Darwin for operation. **"**

My dad's a good tracker too. Just a little while ago some horses were brought to Kalkaringi from Queensland. Soon afterwards they escaped. Horses up here don't need to have shoes and the ground is so dry and rocky that it's hard for *kartiya* to see their footprints. Dad went after those horses and followed their tracks from the settlement, through a fence into the open rocky country and picked them up far away on the other side of the river. It only took him an hour to find them, and they had been gone for quite a while.

Banjo Long is another old stockman who likes to talk about the old days at Wave Hill Station. He still breaks horses at Daguragu and has a small mob of them out there. He has an old stock saddle and all the gear for riding his horses. Banjo is one of the Gurindji who fought in the Second World War.

Banjo Long rides one of his stock horses

Working in Kalkaringi

The Daguragu Community Council Office is in Kalkaringi and is the centre of all council business for Kalkaringi and Daguragu. We usually call it just the "Council Office". The *kartiya* town clerk gets advice from members of the Daguragu Community Council. They make many decisions and have to agree to everything that is done in the community.

The Gurindji do a lot of the work in Kalkaringi, although a number of *kartiya* work here as well, as teachers, health sisters, plumbers and mechanics. There are thirty-five Gurindji people working for the Government – health workers, teachers, clerks, power house operators, plumbers, mechanics, bookkeepers, cleaners, "home-makers", grader drivers and gardeners.

Two *kartiya* health sisters live in Kalkaringi and run the health clinic. They train the Gurindji health workers, who work shifts up at Kalkaringi and down at Daguragu to look after all the people. Every second Tuesday a doctor flies into Kalkaringi to bring in medical supplies and to visit people who are sick. If people need to go to hospital in Katherine or Darwin the medical plane or the mail plane takes them out.

The health workers have a lot to do. The old people need to have regular tests for high blood pressure and diabetes, and once a week the health workers give out tablets to those who need them. Mothers bring their children to be treated at the clinic in the mornings.

Because it's so hot here it's easy to get sores and these must be cleaned and bandaged very often. Little children are weighed and measured to make sure they are growing well. If they are too thin and small, sometimes because they have been sick, they may go on the Skinny Kids programme.

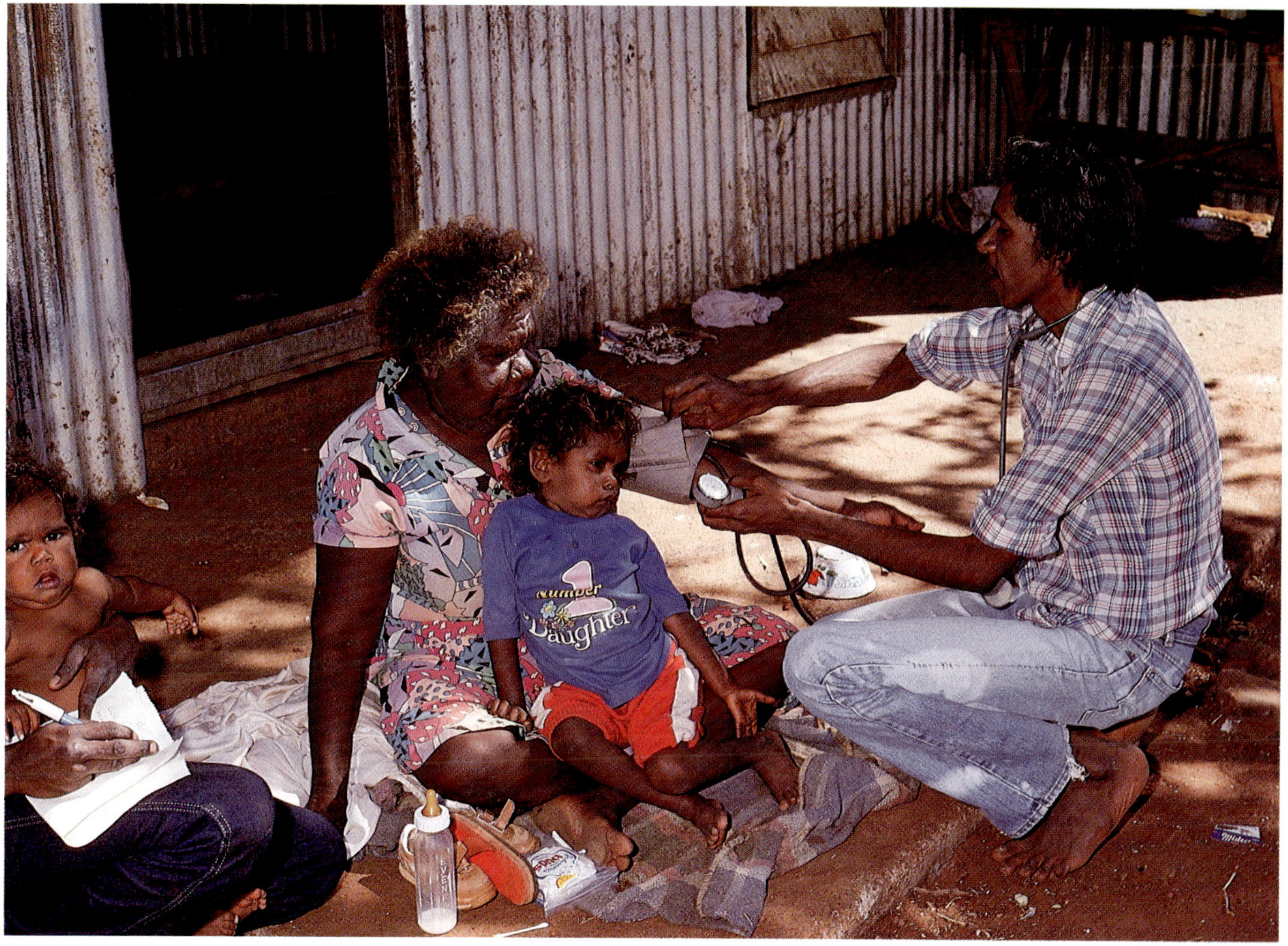

Opposite: My brother Patrick is a health worker at the Daguragu Health Clinic
Above: Here, Patrick checks a woman's blood pressure

Cooking for the skinny kids

The Gurindji Women's Community Group runs the Skinny Kids programme. Every morning at ten o'clock two of the women cook up a good healthy vegetable soup or beef stew, and fruit and custard, to feed the skinny kids. The mothers pay some money and have a plate ready when the women drive around at lunchtime. Usually there are about eight to ten kids on the programme at once. Soon the kids begin to get fatter and after several months they can usually go off the programme.

Some workers in the Gurindji Women's Community Group are called the "home-makers". These women run an old people's kitchen to help the old people who have no family to look after them. They cook one good meal a day for these old people and take it to them in their camps. They help them to have a bath and wash their clothes.

Gus George and Michael Loman run the power house. They are both trained first-class engine drivers. They have to keep the three generators working, look after the power lines, order the diesel fuel from Katherine and always be on call in case the power goes off.

We have a pump house operator too, who looks after the two pumps down on the bore at Wattie Creek to keep the big Kalkaringi water tower full.

Communication

At Kalkaringi and Daguragu we are a long way from the rest of the world. There is no television (but we'll be getting it soon), no medium-wave radio and no current newspapers. People driving in from Katherine sometimes give us news, but we are very isolated.

We can send and receive letters by the mail plane, which flies in from Katherine twice a week, on Wednesdays and Fridays. An hour and a half after leaving Katherine it touches down at Victoria River Downs, the most famous cattle station in the Northern Territory, then later at Wave Hill Station, then Kalkaringi. Then it goes on down to Lajamanu where the Warlpiri people live.

Meeting the mail plane

Wednesday and Friday mornings are busy in the Council Office. All the mail has to be collected and stamped and placed in the big canvas mail bag which hangs just inside the door. At about lunchtime one of the council workers takes the mail out to the airstrip to meet the plane. The council worker and the pilot exchange mail bags. One of the health sisters is usually there, too, to pick up any medical supplies that have been ordered. Every second Wednesday the mail plane brings in cheques for people in the community. The plane holds eight or nine people, so ordinary passengers can fly in and out on the mail plane as well.

The best way of communicating with the outside world is by radio telephone or two-way radio. One of the radio telephones is in the Council Office for everyone to use.

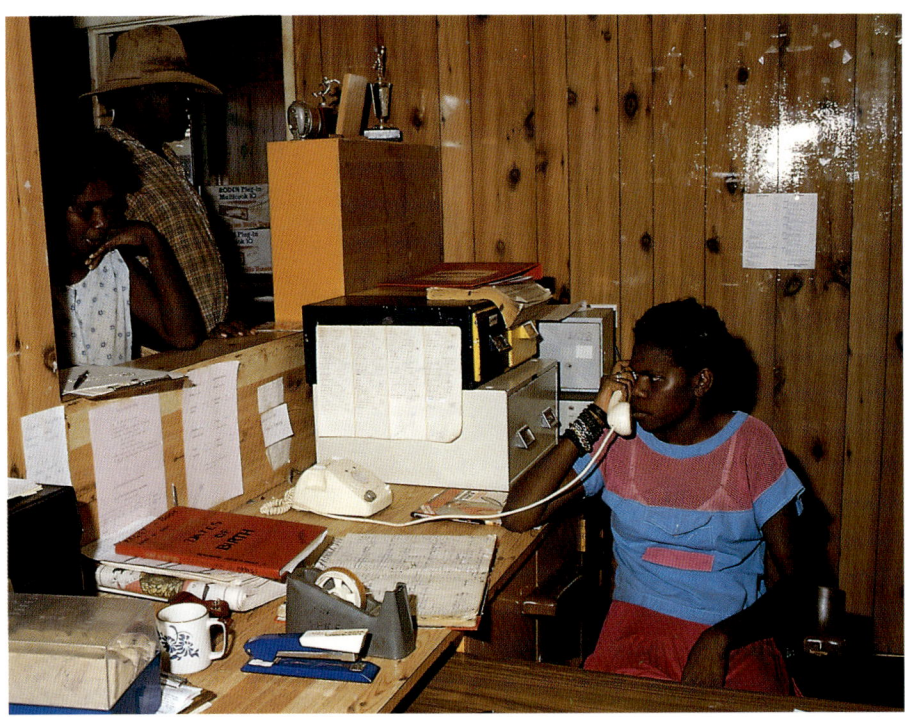

Talking on the radio telephone

It is difficult to make a call on the radio telephone. We sometimes have to wait a long time for the line to be free because the same channel is used all over this part of the Northern Territory. Once we get through to the exchange in Katherine we have to book the call and then wait for the exchange to ring back, maybe two hours later. When we finally reach the person we want to talk to it is very hard to hear the voice on the other end of the line. This is why we only use the radio telephone in emergencies, but the people working in the Council Office have to use it all the time. When a call comes in for someone in Kalkaringi a council worker drives around the town looking for the person who is wanted on the phone.

There are four two-way radios in Kalkaringi — one at the school, one at the police station, one at the health clinic and one at the Baptist mission. There is also one down at Daguragu so that the Wattie Creek health clinic can talk to the Kalkaringi clinic. The health workers need to use the radio to order medical supplies from Katherine, and when there are medical emergencies.

Our School

Kalkaringi School is five minutes' walk from our house. In the cold season we start school at 8.30 and finish at 3.00 but in the dry and wet seasons we start and finish half an hour earlier because it's so hot by early afternoon.

I always try to get to school early so that I can practise on the trampoline before assembly. I am very good at the trampoline. I can jump very high and do lots of tricks. Some of the tricks my friends taught me.

Just after assembly we have morning fitness. It's good fun. The teachers put on some rock music and we do aerobics first, then we all run once around the oval. Some of the teachers run too. The first one back is the winner. I am a fast runner and have been the winner quite a few times.

After morning fitness we all go into class. Year 6 is a small class. There are fifteen boys and four girls. Lance is our *kartiya* teacher. All the other classes in the school have an Aboriginal teacher as well as a *kartiya* teacher and some of their lessons are in Gurindji. They have story books in Gurindji too, which our school librarian made with some of our parents several years ago. They tell some stories from the early days and some stories of life around Kalkaringi today. There are lots of them in the school library and all the kids like to read them.

This year we are doing Language, Maths, Science, Social Studies, Health, Art and Craft, Music, Dance and Drama, and Phys Ed. My favourite subjects are Maths and Phys Ed. I am working hard at school so I can go to Kormilda and train to be a health worker at the Kalkaringi health clinic. When the kids come in with sores I'd like to put the bandages on.

Opposite: *I like to practise on the trampoline before school*
Top: *Morning fitness is good fun*
Below: *Me in class*

Some of my friends are studying to be teachers when they have finished high school. If they pass the interview they will go to Batchelor College to do four years' training. There are several people from our community studying at Batchelor this year. When they are on teaching rounds, they sometimes come home to Kalkaringi to teach in the school.

When we are not in class there is a lot to do at school. Year 6 runs the canteen at morning recess and at lunchtime. We have a roster. The younger kids all line up to buy pies, chips, hot dogs, muesli bars, apples, oranges, mandarins, peanuts and lots of fruit juice drinks.

We also work hard at sport in our spare time. Soccer is our favourite game, which we often play at morning recess, but we also play softball, basketball and football. We practise high jump too. Once a year we have an athletics carnival when we run relay races around the oval, and in the rainy season when the Victoria River is running we have a swimming carnival down on the river.

There are four sports houses in Kalkaringi School – the Yellow Swans, the Blue Bulldogs, the Orange Tigers and the Red Eagles. Your skin name tells you what house you are in. I am in the Yellow Swans with all the other kids whose skin names are *Nalyirri*, *Japalyi*, *Namija* and *Jungurra*. This means that Carolyn, Kerry and I are all in the same house. The Yellow Swans and the Red Eagles are the best houses.

Our Games

After school my friends and I play many games. We often get together with a big group of kids on a spare block to play soccer. The girls and boys all play together and the little kids join in too. We also play hide-and-seek and lots of different skipping games.

Big groups of kids play soccer on a spare block after school

One of our favourite things to do down on the river is to build a slippery slide. You need a lot of kids to make the slide big enough. Usually we choose a steep bank that leads into the river but sometimes we make the slide along the edge of a flat bank. We wet the dry clay along the water's edge and rub it with our hands until it is smooth and slippery. Then we take off most of our clothes and rub ourselves all over with mud from the river. It feels great to have wet, slippery mud all over your body on a hot day. Once the slide is ready – really smooth and slippery – and our bodies are all wet and slippery, we take it in turns to run very fast towards the slide and then slip along it. Sometimes we stay on our feet but usually we slide along on our backs. It is fun, especially when a few kids are sliding at once and we all get tangled up.

We play lots of games in the water too. When our uncles or older cousins come to the river with us we play somersaulting games. We stand in their cupped hands and they fling us straight up in the air. I can do one and a half somersaults before I hit the water, and back flips.

When we feel like quieter games we sometimes strip sheets of bark from the huge paperbark trees along the river and paint on them with red and white clay. We practise some of the traditional patterns the old people have taught us.

Opposite, left: Making a slippery slide on the edge of the waterhole
Opposite, top: We cover ourselves in mud all over
Opposite, bottom: We slide along very fast
Left: Somersaulting is one of our favourite games

Card games are good fun too. My older brothers often play cards with their friends. Mum and Dad like playing cards and sometimes big groups of people get together in the evenings to play. The games go on a long time.

Another good thing for kids to do is disco dancing. Last year some of our teachers organised a Friday night disco down at Daguragu to raise money for Year 6 to go to Sydney and Canberra. (Some of my friends went, but I was only in Year 5 then.) Year 6 made all the food to sell at the disco and everyone paid a dollar to get in. Most of the young people in the community came along. The disco was loads of fun. We had all our favourite music – Dire Straits, Bananarama, Stevie Wonder – and we had disco competitions.

My sisters, my friends and I love to listen to music at home as well. We have a cassette player and lots of tapes. Sometimes when we go into Katherine to buy clothes we come back with new tapes too. I like to spend my money on tapes and earrings best.

Although we don't have television in the settlement yet, lots of people have videos. We have a video player at home and we can hire videos from the take-away in Kalkaringi. Sometimes we have video nights at the school for all the people to watch.

Below: Carol and our friend Beryl listen to Stevie Wonder
Right: The boys play cards in their room

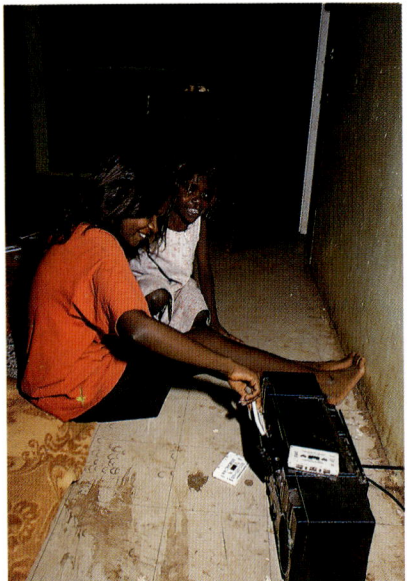

Sport

Sport is very important to the people in Kalkaringi and Daguragu, especially Australian rules football. When it is time for the Grand Final in Melbourne some people even take their short-wave radios out on fishing trips to see if they can get the score. Football fans like to buy videos of the Grand Finals.

Aboriginal people are very good footballers – fast and skilled. There are two Gurindji football teams and the young men train many times a week during the dry season. The teams play against each other and against outsiders. Every Easter there is an Aboriginal football carnival at Barunga, near Katherine, and teams come from all over the Territory. Dad always goes up to Barunga for the Easter carnival.

The Gurindji also have a softball team and three basketball teams – Karungkani, Settlement and Daguragu. My brother Patrick is captain of the Settlement team.

Young boys practising football at Daguragu

The Future

Maybe when my friends and I are older we will be able to go to Sydney and Canberra, and maybe even to Melbourne to watch a Grand Final. I would like to see how other Aboriginal kids and *kartiya* kids live in those big cities. They could show us their special places and we could all talk about our favourite music and movie stars. They could teach us some of their games and we could show them some of ours. I would like to see the ocean too. I've heard about it but it's hard to see it in your mind.

Maybe when I'm a health worker I will visit all those places, but I think I will always come back to Kalkaringi. I am a Gurindji and this is my land. Always.

ACKNOWLEDGEMENTS:

    The author wishes to thank the many people who made this book possible: first and foremost, the Jimmy family of Kalkaringi for their warm hospitality and cooperation; Mick Rangiari, George Kalapiti, Smiler Kata and the Gurindji people of Kalkaringi and Daguragu for their generous support of the project; Helen and Norm McNair, former linguists at Kalkaringi with the Summer Institute of Linguistics, for their helpful criticism of the manuscript and advice on spellings; Erica Hampton, teacher at Kalkaringi School, and Jan Richardson, former town clerk of Kalkaringi, for their support and valuable information; the principal, staff and students of Kalkaringi School for their cooperation; Martin Educational for funding the journey to Kalkaringi; Howard Birnstihl of Northside Productions for his enthusiasm and tireless energy in taking the photographs; and Sally Moss of White Kite Productions for her inspiration and vision for the book.

    Last but not least the author would particularly like to thank her friend Amanda Butler, former teacher at Kalkaringi School, who provided the initial inspiration, who worked so hard to make the idea a reality, and whose special rapport with the Gurindji made the book a possibility in the first place.